TELL ME ABOUT GOD

TELL ME ABOUT GOD

Simple studies in the doctrine of God
for children

Susan Harding

Illustrated by
Lawrence Littleton Evans

THE BANNER OF TRUTH TRUST

THE BANNER OF TRUTH TRUST

3 Murrayfield Road, Edinburgh EH12 6EL
P.O. Box 621, Carlisle, Pennsylvania 17013, USA

★

© The Banner of Truth 1987
First published 1987
ISBN 0 85151 510 X

★

★

Printed and bound
in Great Britain by
McCorquodale (Scotland) Ltd.

For George, Scott and John

Hide – or Seek?

Have you seen very little boys or girls playing hide and seek? Sometimes they shut their eyes and think you can't see them. But of course you can!

Sadly, there are many grown-ups who do the same thing with God. They think that if they say there is no God, God will somehow not be there. But of course God *is* there, and He can see them. Sooner or later, those people will have to explain to God why they have tried to hide from Him; why they have lived as if there was no God; why they have pretended He wasn't there.

There is a God. Everyone knows that really. The important thing is to find out about Him. God commands us to do that: to seek Him. And with that command comes a promise from God specially for boys and girls: those who seek Him early will find Him.

This book is for you, to help you find out what God is like.

About the stories to read

In this book we are trying to learn about GOD. God tells us about Himself in the Bible. In the Old Testament He told His people that His name is 'the Lord'. In the New Testament, Christians said that Jesus Christ is 'the Lord'.

We must not think that the Old Testament is about God the Father, and the New Testament is about God the Son. We must try to understand that the whole Bible is telling us about the one God, Father, Son and Holy Spirit. That is why what you will learn about God in this book is always shown to be true from a New Testament story.

It is hard for us to understand that God is three Persons, but only one God. In this book you will learn different things about God. Those things are true of God the Father, of God the Son, and of God the Holy Spirit. So, God the Father is Almighty, God the Son is Almighty and God the Holy Spirit is Almighty. They are one God.

But you will see, too, that in the great plan of salvation – the Covenant – God the Father makes the plan; God the Son carries it out; and God the Holy Spirit puts it into effect. These three have all agreed together about the plan. Their work is a united work. And They are one God.

About the Bible Songs

Did you know that God has given the Church a hymn-book, right in the middle of your Bible? It is the Book of Psalms.

This is the hymn-book Jesus used when He was here on earth. The psalms were sung every Sabbath day in the synagogue. When He was dying on the cross, Jesus used the words of a psalm as He spoke to His Father: 'Into your hands I commit my spirit.'

When we sing about 'the Lord' in the psalms, we are singing about Christ. Jesus Himself said that the psalms speak about Him. In them, we see Jesus being all the things we learn about God in this book. He is the Lord.

The psalms were the hymn-book of the early Church too. The psalms were sung by men and women who died for Jesus' sake. At the time of the great Reformation of the Church, Christians used to meet together to sing the psalms in fields and parks, in houses and barns.

Nowadays, people have almost forgotten that there is a hymn-book which God Himself has written. It has no mistakes; it will never be out-of-date; and it is what God Himself has given to His Church, so that the Church should worship Him in the right way – His way.

Other hymns are man-made. God's psalms are God-made. Try to learn the Bible-songs (the psalms) in this book. You can sing most of them to any common-metre tune.

God is Almighty

A story to read
Jesus stills the storm. Matthew 8.23-27

A text to learn
You granted him authority over all people, that he might give eternal life to all those you have given him. John 17.2

A Bible song to sing

The storm is changed into a calm
At his command and will,
So that the waves, which raged before
Now quiet are and still.

Then are they glad, because at rest
And quiet now they be;
So to the haven he them brings
Which they desired to see. Psalm 107.29,30

A catechism question
Q.11 What are God's works of providence?
A. God's works of providence are, his most holy, wise, and powerful preserving and governing all his creatures, and all their actions.

God is Almighty

Can the wind blow down a tree? Yes, it can. It is strong. Can the wind blow down a mountain? No, the mountain stops the wind. It is stronger than the wind.

God is stronger than anything. Nothing can stop Him from doing what He wants. Nothing is too hard for Him. He is Almighty.

All God's might and power is given to His Son Jesus Christ. And God has given to Jesus all the sinful people for whom Jesus died. Those people have no power. They are weak. Christ uses all God's might for them. They are rescued, and not one will be lost.

Every Christian is saved and kept safe by God's power in Christ. Ask Him to save and keep you.

God is Blessed

A story to read
The happiness of heaven. Revelation 7.9-17

A text to learn
Blessed are they whose transgressions are forgiven, whose sins are covered. Blessed is the man whose sin the Lord will never count against him. Romans 4.7,8

A Bible song to sing
His name for ever shall endure;
last like the sun it shall:
Men shall be blessed in him, and blessed
all nations shall him call.

Now blessed be the Lord our God,
the God of Israel,
For he alone doth wondrous works,
in glory that excel.

And blessed be his glorious name
to all eternity:
The whole earth let his glory fill.
Amen, so let it be. Psalm 72.17-19

A catechism question
Q.38 What benefits do believers receive from Christ at the resurrection?
A. At the resurrection, believers being raised up in glory, shall be openly acknowledged and acquitted in the day of judgment, and made perfectly blessed in the full enjoying of God to all eternity.

God is Blessed

Are you always happy? Even if something nice happens, are you *really* happy? Only God is really happy, and His happiness never goes away. In the Bible, that happiness is called blessedness. God is blessed for ever.

When the first man was made, he too was happy. He shared in God's blessedness. But when he turned against God, and disobeyed Him, God cursed that man and his family – all of mankind. A curse is the opposite of a blessing. When He curses, God says that bad and sad things will happen. That is why we feel sad deep down.

But for the people whom He had chosen, God promised to take away the curse, and to give a blessing instead!

How can we get that blessing from God? God gives it to everyone who believes in His Son. Only Jesus can make us happy, and take away God's curse from us.

God is the Creator

A story to read
Paul preaches at Athens. Acts 17.16-34

A text to learn
For from him, and through him and to him, are all things. To him be the glory for ever! Amen.
Romans 11.36

A Bible song to sing
To him the spacious sea belongs,
For he the same did make;
The dry land also from his hands
Its form at first did take.

O come and let us worship him,
Let us bow down withal,
And on our knees before the Lord
Our Maker let us fall. Psalm 95.5,6

A catechism question
Q.9 What is the work of creation?
A. The work of creation is God's making all things of nothing, by the word of his power, in the space of six days, and all very good.

God is the Creator

C

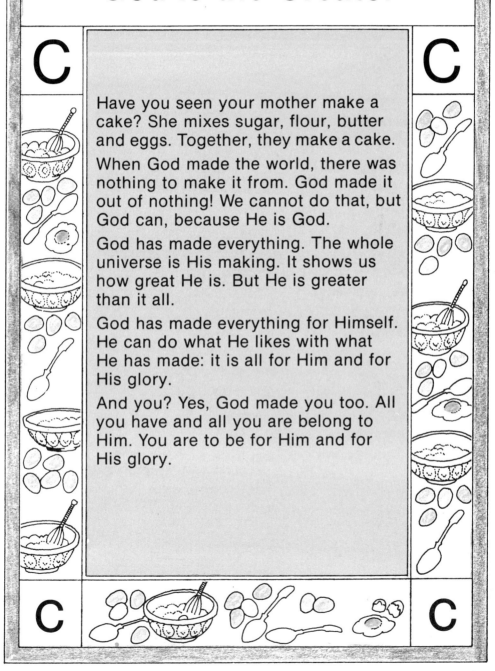

Have you seen your mother make a cake? She mixes sugar, flour, butter and eggs. Together, they make a cake.

When God made the world, there was nothing to make it from. God made it out of nothing! We cannot do that, but God can, because He is God.

God has made everything. The whole universe is His making. It shows us how great He is. But He is greater than it all.

God has made everything for Himself. He can do what He likes with what He has made: it is all for Him and for His glory.

And you? Yes, God made you too. All you have and all you are belong to Him. You are to be for Him and for His glory.

C

C

C

God is the Destroyer of Evil

A story to read
Jesus explains his death. Luke 24.13-35

A text to learn
The reason the Son of God appeared was to destroy the devil's work. 1 John 3.8

A Bible song to sing

Come, and behold what wondrous works
Have by the Lord been wrought;
Come, see what desolations he
Upon the earth hath brought.

Unto the ends of all the earth
Wars into peace he turns:
The bow he breaks, the spear he cuts,
In fire the chariot burns. Psalm 46.8,9

A catechism question
Q.26 How does Christ execute the office of a king?
A. Christ executes the office of a king, in subduing us to himself, in ruling and defending us, and in restraining and conquering all his and our enemies.

God is the Destroyer of Evil

Satan is God's enemy. He is like a snake, destroying things. It was Satan who got the first man, Adam, to sin against God. With that sin came death. Satan was destroying people.

Later, when Jesus became a man, Satan tried to get Jesus to sin, but he could not. Then he got men to kill Jesus. He thought that would destroy Jesus. But instead, when Jesus died, He destroyed Satan!

Because Jesus had no sin, death could not keep hold of Him: He came back to life. And He took away from Satan the power of sin and death.

Now Satan has no power over God's people: he can no longer destroy them. At the end of time, Satan and all those who have served him will be completely destroyed in hell. God will destroy them all.

God is Eternal

A story to read
Jesus and Abraham. John 8.48-59

A text to learn
Now to the King eternal, immortal, invisible, the only God, be honour and glory for ever and ever. Amen. 1 Timothy 1.17

A Bible song to sing
Lord, you have been our dwelling place
In generations all,
Before you ever had brought forth
The mountains great or small.

Ere ever you had formed the earth,
And all the world abroad,
You even from everlasting are
To everlasting, God. Psalm 90.1,2

A catechism question
Q.4 What is God?
A. God is a Spirit, infinite, eternal, and unchangeable in his being, wisdom, power, holiness, justice, goodness, and truth.

God is Eternal

E **E**

Does your mother ever tell you about things which happened before you were born?

There was a time when there was no You – you weren't born; you weren't alive.

But God is different. There was never a time when God was *not* there. God has always been alive.

However far back we think, God was there.

God never changes. He doesn't get old, as we do. He will never die, or go away. He is always there, and always will be.

You can say: I am little. I will be big.

But God says: I am who I am. That is what His name Jehovah, THE LORD means.

e **e**

God is Faithful

A story to read
The Lord's Supper. Mark 14.12-26

A text to learn
Know that the Lord your God is God; he is the faithful God, keeping his covenant of love to a thousand generations of those who love him and keep his commands. Deuteronomy 7.9

A Bible song to sing
I'll make him my first born, more high
Than kings of any land;
My love I'll ever keep for him,
My covenant fast shall stand. Psalm 89.27,28

Yet I'll not take my love from him
Nor false my promise make.
My covenant I'll not break, nor change
What with my mouth I spake. Psalm 89.33,34

A catechism question
Q.92 What is a sacrament?
A. A sacrament is a holy ordinance instituted by Christ, wherein, by sensible signs, Christ and the benefits of the New Covenant, are represented, sealed, and applied to believers.

God is Faithful

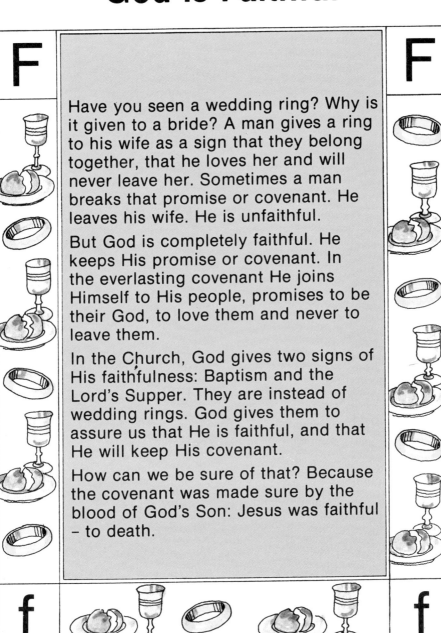

Have you seen a wedding ring? Why is it given to a bride? A man gives a ring to his wife as a sign that they belong together, that he loves her and will never leave her. Sometimes a man breaks that promise or covenant. He leaves his wife. He is unfaithful.

But God is completely faithful. He keeps His promise or covenant. In the everlasting covenant He joins Himself to His people, promises to be their God, to love them and never to leave them.

In the Church, God gives two signs of His faithfulness: Baptism and the Lord's Supper. They are instead of wedding rings. God gives them to assure us that He is faithful, and that He will keep His covenant.

How can we be sure of that? Because the covenant was made sure by the blood of God's Son: Jesus was faithful – to death.

God is Glorious

A story to read
The transfiguration. Matthew 17.1-8

A text to learn
Father, I want those you have given me to be with me where I am, and to see my glory, the glory you have given me because you loved me before the creation of the world. John 17.24

A Bible song to sing
For God the Lord's a sun and shield:
He'll grace and glory give;
And will withhold no good from them
That uprightly do live. Psalm 84.11

A catechism question
Q.37 What benefits do believers receive from Christ at death?
A. The souls of believers are at their death made perfect in holiness, and do immediately pass into glory, and their bodies, being still united to Christ, do rest in their graves till the resurrection.

God is Glorious

Have you seen the sun setting? Nothing else is so splendid. That is the glory which belongs just to the sun. Sometimes though, the sun's glory is hidden by the clouds. The glory is still there, but we cannot see it.

God has a far greater glory than the sun. But people do not see it: it is hidden from them because of their sin.

How can we see God's glory? By repenting and learning what God is like. Jesus shows us that. When we learn what Jesus is like, we see God's glory. We can see this a little bit now, but in heaven Christians will see Christ face to face. They will be in glory.

The moon has no light of its own. It shines back the sun's light. Christians have no glory of their own. They should reflect the glory of Christ.

God is the Holy One

A story to read
Part of Jesus' great prayer. John 17.15-19

A text to learn
It is written: Be holy, because I am holy.
1 Peter 1.16

A Bible song to sing (about the Son of David)

For to the Lord belongs our shield,
That does us safety bring;
And unto Israel's Holy One
The man that is our king.

In vision to your Holy One
You said, I help upon
A strong one laid; out of the folk
I raised a chosen one.

Even David, I have found him out
A servant unto me;
And with my holy oil my King
Anointed him to be. Psalm 89.18-20

A catechism question
Q.35 What is sanctification?
A. Sanctification is the work of God's free grace,
by which we are renewed in the whole man after
the image of God, and are enabled more and
more to die to sin, and live to righteousness.

God is the Holy One

 **H**

 **H**

Has your mother got a precious vase or glass? I'm sure she keeps it in a special place, away from ordinary things like pots and pans. It is special.

God is extra special, because He alone is God. There is no-one at all like Him. He is so special that He is set apart from everything else. He is the HOLY ONE.

We sinners have no idea of how holy God is. God has put Himself far, far away from sin. He will have nothing to do with it. He is Holy.

God commands you to get away from sin. He sets His people on one side for His own special use. Ask Him to make you holy.

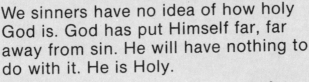

 h

 **h**

God is the Inspirer

A story to read
The eunuch of Ethiopia. Acts 8.26-40

A text to learn
The Spirit gives life; the flesh counts for nothing.
The words I have spoken to you are spirit and
they are life. John 6.63

A Bible song to sing

Let your sweet mercies also come
And visit me, O Lord;
Let your salvation come to me
According to your word.

According to your faithful word
Uphold and stablish me,
That I may live, and of my hope
Ashamèd never be. Psalm 119.41 and 116

A catechism question
Q.89 How is the word made effectual to salvation?
A. The Spirit of God makes the reading, but
especially the preaching of the word, an effectual
means of convincing and converting sinners, and
of building them up in holiness and comfort,
through faith, to salvation.

God is the Inspirer

When God made the first man, He breathed His Spirit of life into him: the man became a living soul.

When someone writes a book, he puts down words to say something. When God wrote His special book, the Bible, He made certain men His messengers. They wrote down God's own word, and as they wrote, God breathed life into the words: the Bible is the living word. It is quite different from any other book. It is God-breathed, it is full of life. It is inspired.

When God speaks to sinners, He speaks in the Bible, by His Spirit. That is how He brings them back to life again, when they had been dead in sin.

God is the Judge

A story to read
A time of judgment. Revelation 11.15-19

A text to learn
Lord God Almighty, true and just are your judgments. Revelation 16.7

A Bible song to sing
The Lord for ever does endure;
For judgment sets his throne;
In righteousness to judge the world,
Justice to give each one. Psalm 9.7,8

A catechism question
Q.85 What does God require of us, that we may escape his wrath and curse due to us for sin?
A. To escape the wrath and curse of God due to us for sin, God requires of us faith in Jesus Christ, repentance unto life, with the diligent use of all the outward means by which Christ communicates to us the benefits of redemption.

God is the Judge

J

God is the perfect judge. His laws tell us what is right and wrong.

God is never unfair. He judges rich and poor alike. He knows everything. He knows what people have done and even what they think.

God carries out His laws. He will always punish what is bad, and reward what is good. All sin will be punished by God. Everyone who sins is guilty. We have all sinned except Jesus.

The sins of God's people were punished too. Jesus was punished, instead of those people. He died for everyone who asks for His forgiveness.

You are a sinner. Ask Jesus to forgive you. If you don't, God will judge you.

J

j

j

God is King

A story to read
Saul's conversion. Acts 9.1-19

A text to learn
Those who obey his commands live in him, and he in them. And this is how we know that he lives in us: We know it by the Spirit he gave us.
1 John 3.24

A Bible song to sing
Your arrows sharply pierce the heart
Of the enemies of the King;
And under your dominion they
The people down do bring.

For ever and for ever is,
O God, your throne of might;
The sceptre of your kingdom is
A sceptre that is right. Psalm 45.5-6

A catechism question
Q.87 What is repentance unto life?
A. Repentance unto life is a saving grace, by which a sinner, out of a true sense of his sin and apprehension of the mercy of God in Christ, does, with grief and hatred of his sin, turn from it to God, with full purpose of, and endeavour after, new obedience.

God is King

A king is someone who tells other people what he wants them to do, and who is able to make them do it.

God is the great King. He has a kingdom. It is made up of those people who do what He tells them. They are scattered all over the world. They cannot see their King. How do they know what He wants them to do? He has told them, in the Bible.

When God brings people into His kingdom He gives them His Holy Spirit. The Holy Spirit changes those people. Before, they had disobeyed God. Now, they want to obey Him: they begin to love doing what He says.

God is a King in His people's lives. His laws tell them what He wants done. His Spirit gives His people the will to do it. So what God wants is done: He is King.

God is Love

A story to read
The Good Samaritan. Luke 10.25-37

A text to learn
For God so loved the world that he gave his one and only Son, that whoever believes in him shall not perish but have eternal life. John 3.16

A Bible song to sing

As far as east is distant from
The west, so far has he
From us removèd, in his love,
All our iniquity.

Such pity as a father has
Unto his children dear,
Like pity shows the Lord to such
As worship him in fear. Psalm 103.12,13

A catechism question
Q.34 What is adoption?
A. Adoption is an act of God's free grace, by which we are received into the number, and have a right to all the privileges, of the sons of God.

God is Love

Do you love ice-cream? If you do, it is because the taste pleases you – you like it, because it is nice.

God's love is different. He doesn't love people because they please Him. All the people in this world are sinful: they are not nice to God.

When God loves, He makes up His mind to do something good. Love is not just a feeling God has: it is when He comes to help. God's love is when He does something good to something bad.

The Bible tells us how God loved the world which hated Him. He loved it so much that He did something good to it: He gave it the most precious thing He had: His own Son, Jesus. Only He could do any good to the world. He could make the bad good.

If we love God, it is because He first loved us.

God is Merciful

A story to read
The repentant thief. Luke 23.32-43

A text to learn
I will have mercy on whom I have mercy. And I will have compassion on whom I have compassion. Romans 9.15

A Bible song to sing
Your tender mercies, Lord,
To mind do you recall,
And loving-kindnesses, for they
Have been through ages all.

My sins and faults of youth
Do you, O Lord, forget:
After your mercy, think on me,
And for your goodness great. Psalm 25.6,7

A catechism question
Q.20 Did God leave all mankind to perish in the estate of sin and misery?
A. God having, out of his mere good pleasure, from all eternity, elected some to everlasting life, did enter into a covenant of grace, to deliver them out of the estate of sin and misery, and to bring them into an estate of salvation by a Redeemer.

God is Merciful

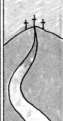

Supposing two bullies were to beat you up. Which one would you give your birthday present to? Neither! Neither of them deserved any kindness from you.

Can you see how we are like that, to God? Of course, we can't really bully GOD. But we try to: we think we can order Him around and get away with it. So there is no reason why God should be kind to *anyone*.

There is no reason why He should be – except that God is merciful. In Christ, He chooses to show mercy to some: to pick them out, to forgive them, to love them, to give them His Son. He chose to save them even before He made the world.

Unbelievers say: God ought to choose everybody.

But believers pray: "Lord, have mercy on me, a sinner." They are the ones who belong to Jesus, and for them Jesus died.

God is a Near Relative

A story to read
The raising of Lazarus. John 11.1-43

A text to learn
The life I live in the body, I live by faith in the Son of God, who loved me and gave himself for me. Galatians 2.20

A Bible song to sing
O Lord, my soul you have brought up,
And rescued from the grave;
That I to death should not go down,
Alive you did me save. Psalm 30.3

A catechism question
Q.21 Who is the Redeemer of God's elect?
A. The only Redeemer of God's elect is the Lord Jesus Christ who, being the eternal Son of God, became man, and so was, and continues to be, God and man in two distinct natures and one person, for ever.

God is a Near Relative

When someone whom we love dies, we feel very sad. However much we loved that person, we couldn't stop him dying. We couldn't die instead of him. Each person must die for himself. That is part of the punishment for sin. Each person has his own sin to pay for.

Only one person had no sins to pay for: Jesus Christ. He never sinned. He did not need to die. But God the Father had made a plan (or covenant) with His Son, Jesus, that He should die for those people God had loved and chosen. Jesus loved them too. So He became their nearest relative and friend: their Redeemer. He paid the price for their sins: He redeemed them. He died instead of them.

Christians' bodies still die. But even they are redeemed, and will be made perfect at the resurrection.

God is Over All Things

A story to read

A miraculous catch of fish. John 21.1-14

A text to learn

Jesus came to them and said, "All authority in heaven and on earth has been given to me. Therefore go and make disciples of all nations, baptising them in the name of the Father and of the Son and of the Holy Spirit, and teaching them to obey everything I have commanded you. And surely I will be with you always, to the very end of the age." Matthew 28.18-20

A Bible song to sing

The Lord builds up Jerusalem,
And he it is alone
That the dispersed of Israel
Does gather into one. Psalm 147.2

A catechism question

Q.7 What are the decrees of God?
A. The decrees of God are his eternal purpose, according to the counsel of his will, whereby, for his own glory, he has fore-ordained whatsoever comes to pass.

God is Over All Things

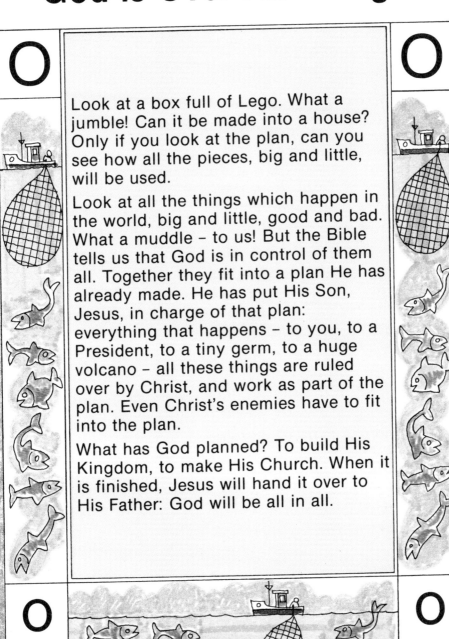

Look at a box full of Lego. What a jumble! Can it be made into a house? Only if you look at the plan, can you see how all the pieces, big and little, will be used.

Look at all the things which happen in the world, big and little, good and bad. What a muddle – to us! But the Bible tells us that God is in control of them all. Together they fit into a plan He has already made. He has put His Son, Jesus, in charge of that plan: everything that happens – to you, to a President, to a tiny germ, to a huge volcano – all these things are ruled over by Christ, and work as part of the plan. Even Christ's enemies have to fit into the plan.

What has God planned? To build His Kingdom, to make His Church. When it is finished, Jesus will hand it over to His Father: God will be all in all.

God is our Peace

A story to read
The Lord and Zacchaeus. Luke 19.1-10

A text to learn
He was pierced for our transgressions, he was crushed for our iniquities; the punishment that brought us peace was upon him, and by his wounds we are healed. Isaiah 53.5

A Bible song to sing
I'll hear what God the Lord will speak;
To his folk he'll speak peace,
And to his saints; but let them not
Return to foolishness.

Truth meets with mercy, righteousness
And peace kiss mutually;
Truth springs from earth, and righteousness
Looks down from heaven high. Psalm 85.8,10

A catechism question
Q.25 How does Christ execute the office of a priest?
A. Christ executes the office of a priest, in his once offering up of himself a sacrifice to satisfy divine justice and reconcile us to God; and in making continual intercession for us.

God is our Peace

God is at peace with Himself. He is three Persons in one God, and those three Persons always agree with each other. They work together perfectly. They never quarrel. They are at peace.

We are not like that. We are not at peace with others: we quarrel.

We are not at peace in ourselves: one part of us wants one thing, another part wants something else.

We are not at peace with God; we disagree with what He says. We deliberately work against Him. We are His enemies.

But God had a peace-plan: His covenant, that Christ should make peace between God and His enemies, by His death on the cross. To those people who believe in Him, Christ gives His peace. They become at peace with God, with others, and with themselves.

But there is no peace for the wicked.

God is the Questioner

A story to read
The woman at the well. John 4.1-26

A text to learn
Godly sorrow brings repentance that leads to salvation and leaves no regret, but worldly sorrow brings death. 2 Corinthians 7.10

A Bible song to sing

Lord, you have searched me, and have known
My rising up and lying down;
And from afar your searching eye
Beholds my thoughts that secret lie.

Search me, O God, my heart discern,
Try me, my very thoughts to learn;
See if in evil paths I stray,
And guide me in the eternal way. Psalm 139.1,15

A catechism question
Q.14 What is sin?
A. Sin is any want of conformity unto, or transgression of, the law of God.

God is the Questioner

Q Q

God does not need to ask people questions: He knows everything already. He even knows what we are thinking. But still, God is the questioner. It is good when He searches us.

When God questions us, He does it to show up how we are always making excuses, or blaming someone else; or saying we are right and God is wrong. All our excuses are shown up as frauds.

God reasons with us, so that we should change our minds (repent). We need to know for sure that we are sinners, and that we must put our trust in Christ. We must do this now.

When the world ends, everyone must face God. God will still be the questioner. He will ask each person to answer for what he or she has done in this life. If we have not trusted in Christ in this life, every answer we give will show us up as guilty.

q  q

God is our Righteousness

A story to read
The wedding garment. Matthew 22.1-14

A text to learn
This righteousness from God comes through faith in Jesus Christ to all who believe. Romans 3.22

A Bible song to sing
And I will constantly go on
In strength of God the Lord;
And your own righteousness, even yours
Alone, I will record. Psalm 71.16

A catechism question
Q.33 What is justification?
A. Justification is an act of God's free grace by which he pardons all our sins and accepts us as righteous in his sight, only for the righteousness of Christ imputed to us, and received by faith alone.

God is our Righteousness

 R R

God always does what is right. He never does anything wrong. God loves what is right. He hates what is evil.

All God's righteousness is shown to us in Jesus' life on earth. Every day Jesus did what was right. He did nothing wrong.

Each day we sin. We do not love what is good or hate what is bad. We have no righteousness.

What can we do about that? How can we be right enough for God? We can do nothing. All our righteousness is like dirty rags.

But God gives to His people all the righteousness of Jesus. Only that is good enough for God. Jesus is the righteousness of God for those who believe in Him.

r   r

God is Sovereign

A story to read
Jesus frees the mad man. Luke 8.26-39

A text to learn
I tell you the truth, everyone who sins is a slave to sin ... If the Son sets you free, you will be free indeed. John 8.34,36

A Bible song to sing
He out of darkness did them bring
And from death's shade them take;
Their bands, wherewith they had been bound
He did asunder break. Psalm 107.14

A catechism question
Q.31 What is effectual calling?
A. Effectual calling is the work of God's Spirit, whereby, convincing us of our sin and misery, enlightening our minds in the knowledge of Christ, and renewing our wills, he persuades and enables us to embrace Jesus Christ, freely offered to us in the gospel.

God is Sovereign

Have you seen a toddler in a temper? It wants something, but its mother says 'No'. The child has a strong will. But its mother's will is stronger, and she is in charge of the child.

All people are born with a will: the part of them which decides what they want. But nobody's will is free to decide to want God. Because of sin, people always decide that they don't want God and they don't want to obey Him.

But God is sovereign. He too has a will. God's will is stronger than ours, and He is in charge of us.

God's will is that His people are to be saved. It is His sovereign purpose. Nothing can stop it. People say: "We don't want God." But, if God has chosen them, His Spirit changes their wills: He sets them free. Then they say: "I want to believe in Christ, I want to love and obey Him. I want to!"

God is the Truth

A story to read
The Pharisee and the publican. Luke 18.9-14

A text to learn
If we claim to be without sin, we deceive ourselves and the truth is not in us. 1 John 1.8

A Bible song to sing
O let the way of falsehood far
From me removèd be;
And graciously your holy law
Do you grant unto me.

I chosen have the perfect way
Of truth and verity:
Your judgments that most righteous are
Before me laid have I. Psalm 119.29,30

A catechism question
Q.84 What does every sin deserve?
A. Every sin deserves God's wrath and curse, both in this life and in that which is to come.

God is the Truth

T   T

Why do we tell lies? Usually because we have done something wrong – and we don't want anyone to find out.

God always tells the truth. He has never done anything wrong. When God speaks about Himself He has nothing to hide or to be ashamed of.

When we think about ourselves we often pretend – even to ourselves – that we are better than we are. But God never pretends. He really is what He says. God is so good that He alone is pleased with what He is. He is the truth.

God tells the truth about us. He tells us we are sinners, and that we must agree with and trust all that He says.

t   t

God is Unsearchable

A story to read
The Pharisees confounded. Luke 20.1-8

A text to learn
I live in a high and holy place, but also with him who is contrite and lowly in spirit. Isaiah 57.15

A Bible song to sing

Now for your own name's sake,
O Lord, I you entreat
To pardon my iniquity
For it is very great.

What man is he that fears
The Lord, and does him serve?
Him shall he teach the way that he
Shall choose, and still observe.

With those that fear him is
The secret of the Lord;
The knowledge of his covenant
He will to them afford. Psalm 25.11,12,14

A catechism question (a truth we may not question)
Q.19 What is the misery of that estate into which man fell?
A. All mankind by their fall lost communion with God, are under his wrath and curse, and so made liable to all miseries in this life, to death itself, and to the pains of hell for ever.

God is Unsearchable

U   U

God may search us, and ask us questions. But we may not do that to God. There are some things God does not choose to tell us. We must not pry into those things. There are other things we do not understand, because our thinking is dulled by sin. We must not question what God does.

Proud men like to think God must explain all He does to them. But God is against people who proudly question Him. He is the sinless One who decides what is right. How can sinful people judge a sinless God?

God is unsearchable – beyond our finding out. Yet He makes His home with humble people who are sorry for their sins. They do not question God, or what He does. And to them, God shows His secrets.

u   u

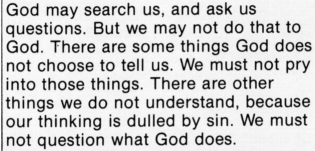

God is the Vindicator

A story to read
The parable of the persistent widow. Luke 18.1-8

A text to learn
Do not take revenge, my friends, but leave room for God's wrath, for it is written, "It is mine to avenge; I will repay", says the Lord. Romans 12.19

A Bible song to sing (about the wicked)

Against the righteous souls they join,
They guiltless blood condemn.
But of my refuge God's the rock,
And my defence from them.

On them their own iniquity
The Lord shall cause to fall,
And in their sin shall cut them off;
Our God destroy them shall. Psalm 94.21-23

A catechism question
Q.102 What do we pray for in the second petition (of the Lord's prayer)?
A. In the second petition (which is, Your kingdom come) we pray, that Satan's kingdom may be destroyed; and that the kingdom of grace may be advanced, ourselves and others brought into it, and kept in it; and that the kingdom of glory may be hastened.

God is the Vindicator

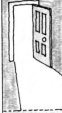

Do you believe in God? Remember, He is the God we cannot see. Many people don't believe in Him. They say, "Show us your God." Sometimes they say, "There is no God. We can prove it." Sometimes they hurt Christians, or tell lies about them, or even kill them.

Will God let them get away with that? No! God Himself will show that believers are right: that His Word is true. He will vindicate them.

Now, people think Christians are on the losing side: they can't see their Captain. But He is Christ, and God cannot lose.

When Jesus comes back to earth at the end of time, the unseen God will show Himself. Then everyone will see Him. God will make His enemies see that Jesus is the Lord; that what He said was right; that what Christians believed was true. And every unbeliever will be punished.

God is the Word

A story to read
Jesus reads at Nazareth. Luke 4.14-30

A text to learn
In the beginning was the Word, and the Word was with God, and the Word was God ... the Word became flesh and lived for a while among us. John 1.1,14

A Bible song to sing
The mighty God, the Lord,
Speaks, and to earth does call,
Even from the rising of the sun
To where it has its fall.

From out of Zion hill
Where beauty dwells enshrined
God in his glorious majesty
And mighty power has shined. Psalm 50.1,2

A catechism question
Q.24 How does Christ execute the office of a prophet?
A. Christ executes the office of a prophet in revealing to us, by his word and Spirit, the will of God for our salvation.

God is the Word

Have you ever seen a new baby? God made it. This teaches us how good God is, and that He is kind to us.

All the things God has made teach us He is good. Why don't we love and praise Him then? Because sin has spoilt us and our thinking.

God knew that sinful people would need to be taught by something more than the things God had made. So God Himself became our teacher. He spoke to people at different times, and He always spoke to them through His Son. Jesus is the Word of God – God speaking to us. Jesus became a man Himself, so that He could speak to people face to face.

Listen to Him when you read your Bible!

God is eXcellent

A story to read
Man-made religion condemned. Matthew 15.1-20

A text to learn
God is spirit, and his worshippers must worship in spirit and in truth. John 4.24

A Bible song to sing

The praises of your wonders, Lord,
The heavens shall express;
The assembly of the holy ones
Shall praise your faithfulness.

For who in heaven with the Lord
May once himself compare?
Who is like God among the sons
Of those that mighty are?

Great fear in meeting of the saints
Is due unto the Lord;
And he above all round him should
With reverence be adored. Psalm 89.5-7

A catechism question
Q.46 What is required in the first commandment?
A. The first commandment requires us to know and acknowledge God to be the only true God, and our God; and to worship and glorify him accordingly.

God is eXcellent

X   X

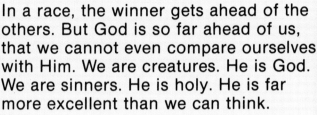

In a race, the winner gets ahead of the others. But God is so far ahead of us, that we cannot even compare ourselves with Him. We are creatures. He is God. We are sinners. He is holy. He is far more excellent than we can think.

We praise God for what He is. But we must be careful that we know what God is really like. We must have the right ideas about Him: the things God tells us about Himself in the Bible. If we think our own ideas about God, they will be wrong. Then we would be praising a god we've made-up ourselves: that would be worshipping an idol.

When we praise God, using His own word in the psalms, we can be sure we are worshipping the true God. They tell God how excellent He is, how excellent the things are He has made and done.

X   X

God is "Yes" and "Amen"

A story to read
Christ and believers: the Vine and its branches.
John 15.5-8

A text to learn
No matter how many promises God has made, they are "Yes" in Christ. And so through him the "Amen" is spoken by us to the glory of God.
2 Corinthians 1.20

A Bible song to sing
All blessing to the Lord our God
Let be ascribèd then:
For evermore so let it be,
Amen, Yes, and Amen. Psalm 89.52

A catechism question
Q.36 What are the benefits which in this life accompany or flow from justification, adoption and sanctification?
A. The benefits which in this life accompany or flow from justification, adoption and sanctification are assurance of God's love, peace of conscience, joy in the Holy Ghost, increase of grace, and perseverance therein to the end.

God is "Yes" and "Amen"

Y Y

Do you know how much your parents looked forward to having a baby – even before you were born? And now, they often look back to when you were born. All that happiness comes to them, in you!

From the beginning, God taught His people to *look forward* to when He would send a Saviour. In the Old Testament, God's people believed that promise: they looked forward to, and hoped for, the Saviour.

God made many other promises, and they all depended on the great promise of a Saviour. God would only bless people, and be their God, because of what the Saviour would do.

Now we *look back* to when Jesus came. All God's promises are given in Jesus and what He did. Because of Him, God says "Yes and Amen" to every one of them. Christ has made every promise absolutely sure. "Amen" means "Sure"! All those promises come to believers, in Christ.

y  y

God is Zealous

A story to read
Jesus cleanses the temple. John 2.12-25

A text to learn
My food, said Jesus, is to do the will of him who sent me, and to finish his work. John 4.34

A Bible song to sing
For I have borne reproach for you,
My face is clothed with shame,
To brethren strange, to mother's sons
An alien I became.

Because the zeal did eat me up
Which to your house I bear,
And the reproaches cast at you
Upon me fallen are. Psalm 69.7-9

A catechism question
Q.27 Wherein did Christ's humiliation consist?
A. Christ's humiliation consisted in his being born, and that in a low condition, made under the law, undergoing the miseries of this life, the wrath of God, and the cursed death of the cross; in being buried, and continuing under the power of death for a time.

God is Zealous

We are often lazy, but even when we work hard we are not always certain what to do, or we get tired or give up.

When Christ was here on earth, He knew exactly what He was meant to do: He kept covenant perfectly with God, working out His Father's plan, doing His will. He was never lazy: He spent all His life working for His Father. He was never weak: the Holy Spirit strengthened Him. He never changed His mind, or gave up what He was doing. He knew what He had to do – and He did it. This meant being tired, hungry, despised and lonely. Doing what God wanted even meant dying.

Jesus said: "Zeal for your house has consumed me."

If you belong to God's house (the Church) then it was for you that Christ was consumed (used up). Ask Him to make you zealous. Use yourself up, for Him.

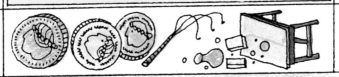